A view from the bandstand

Greta Kent

The text was compiled by Carole Spedding,
from Greta Kent's writings and from conversations with her
at her Suffolk home.

Sheba Feminist Publishers

British Library Cataloguing in Publication Data

Kent, Greta
   A view from the bandstand.
   1. Women musicians   2. Bands (Music)
   I. Title
   785'.06'60924   MT733

The author and publishers wish to thank Mrs Pitt and Mr Dennis
Egan for the loan of photographs from their private collections.
Thanks, also, to all of Greta Kent's family for their untiring support
and encouragement and to Jill Nicholls for her help with editing.

Cover photo – The Grosvenor Ladies' Quintette

A View from the Bandstand first published in 1983 by Sheba Feminist
Publishers, 488 Kingsland Road, London E8 4AE.

Designed by Susan Hobbs and Hilary Arnott
Typeset by Range Left (TU) 01-251 3959
All rights reserved   ©
ISBN 0 907179 19 3
Printed by A. Wheaton & Co. Ltd, Exeter

This book is dedicated to all the lady musicians in my family, and to the other lady musicians that I knew. And also to those in the past that I didn't know. Because, of course, I didn't get to know them all.

Greta Kent as a teenager. Approximately 1910.

Many of us assume that women's bands in this country are an invention of the contemporary women's movement. Not so. Before the turn of the century and for quite some time afterwards 'Ladies' Orchestras' were a regular fixture at holiday resorts, teashops, pavilions and concert halls. For example, when J. Lyons opened his very first Cornerhouse in 1909 at The Strand, London, these groups of professional and skilled lady musicians regularly provided entertainment for the customers.

Sometimes they played in duos or trios but just as often orchestras of thirty or more played at special events, such as trade exhibitions and the Ideal Home Exhibitions at Earls Court. Playing all the popular airs of the time they earned their living by travelling the country, and sometimes abroad. The situation changed with the import of 'Talkies' and 'Jazz' bands to Britain, but in their heyday these Ladies Orchestras were well known and respected.

The photographs in this book come from just one family album showing us what a hardworking but enjoyable life the ladies of the Kent and Baldwin families had. Through their story we gain an insight into a chapter of women's history, and the history of music, that had almost been forgotten. ■

↑
Mother

Much has been written about the entertainment world: the theatre with its famous actresses and actors, films, circuses and even Punch and Judy shows. But what would the Music Halls and 'Variety Turns' have been without the bands? Without the soft, prolonged roll on the snare drum as the acrobat balanced on one arm at the apex of a human pyramid and the 'back chat' of the conductor with the comedians? And what would the theatre of that time have been without the overture and curtain raiser to set the mood of the play?

The lady players who worked so diligently in these orchestras also created their own separate reputation. Yet no one has attempted to make noticeable mention of Ladies' Orchestras, so tremendously popular in their day. Why not, I wonder? Were they or are they not important enough to be worthy of comment, or has the pleasure they gave long since been forgotten? Let me, then, remind readers a little of those days . . .

I was born in Wimbledon in 1895. Long before I came on the scene ladies had been forming small groups for musical evenings, mostly for their own entertainment. Pianos, cellos, and violins were the usual instruments chosen until a vogue was started for the mandolin.

My first recollection of seeing ladies in orchestras was when I was taken on tour with my parents. Father was then Musical Director of an operetta entitled 'The Red Spider', an adaptation of a book by the Rev. Baring Gould. Mother was also playing, by now on trombone, and there was a lady harpist. I was then between three and four years old. The next I call to mind was a holiday spent in Lowestoft with two young aunts who were engaged to play in a concert party. It must have been a high class affair to have had a musical quartet.

Both my mother and father were musicians and earned their living from it. My mother, Nellie Baldwin, was a good pianist and violinist before she broke with tradition for lady musicians and took to playing the trombone. She sometimes played with father in mixed orchestras and sometimes just with other ladies.

A special luncheon party for lady musicians given by Sir Edward Elgar. Probably in the early 1920s. It was a very special occasion. I remember that I was away at the time and Mother wrote to me saying, 'We've all been to a luncheon party that Sir Edward Elgar was giving.' They look rather elegant don't they? These ladies are from different orchestras but many of them must have known each other very well and have worked together. Some may have been disengaged at the time, but some must have been enjoying engagements and managed the time to come up to London just for this special luncheon. Elgar was always very nice to the ladies.

Mother playing the guitar, second left, in a very early band. This was taken before she started playing wind instruments, so it must have been in the very early 1880s.

Grandmother Baldwin's Anglo Saxon Ladies' Band. This is the earliest photograph that we have in our family album. Grandmother is seated second left, Mother on her left with the violin, and Aunt Hilda standing left with the cornet. This must have been taken about 1880 if not a little before.

Her mother, my Grandmother Baldwin, was a very good musician and must have foreseen something of the future attraction to the public of Ladies' Orchestras. She had her own group called The Anglo Saxon Ladies Band (above) which included flute, clarinet and cornet.

When her daughter, my mother, met and married Ernest Kent in early 1893, he was already making his living from the violin. He had started playing when very young. He would play at balls, private parties, receptions and at theatres for operas and musical comedies. The hardworking, qualified and skilled instrumentalists with whom he worked in these orchestras gave a contribution to the theatre that was as important to the production as the scenery, the costumes and even the acting.

Later, Father took up conducting too – he was Resident Conductor at the Grand Theatre, Luton, for six years from 1900.

When we returned to London he was engaged at some variety theatres of the Moss Empires and the Gulliver Circuits.

And *his* father, my Grandfather John Caswell Kent, had a good knowledge of the bass as well as the fiddle and had his own orchestras such as the one at Roshville Gardens, Gravesend, in 1889. Gardens were popular resorts for entertainment in those days and the weather *always* seemed right!

Others of Grandfather's family were employed there – two sons playing viola and violin while two of his three daughters danced and sang. He also taught these daughters to play the cornet while the third became very polished indeed on the trombone. They all became expert enough to join other important acts later in life (see special section page 39). So two fine musical families united when my mother and father married.

9

*Grandfather Kent
as a child.*

Right: Grandfather Kent . . . later. He was a trumpet major in the 14th Dragoons (1846) and his book of manuscript pieces arranged for special occasions is still extant. He was also a foremost performer on the cornet, noted particularly for his 'triple-tonguing' (the ability to play rapidly each note three times thus producing triplets). Not all of Grandfather's ventures were successful – some diary entries state mishaps such as 'came to grief here', and I feel that Grandmother, with her seven or eight offspring, must have had many financial worries, which she appears to have weathered well. When Grandfather told us children that he had been a soldier, a sailor and a policeman, we laughed with him unbelievingly but on going through his notebooks I see what he meant, for he was Bandmaster of the 3rd Middlesex Militia in 1875, Bandmaster onboard HMS Spartan and he held the same position in the P Division of Police in 1881. This must mean that in those days musicians could move around from one institution to another for employment whereas I don't think that is possible these days.

Undoubtedly Grandfather Kent was an interesting and colourful character, always busy, never seeming bored, and always ready to amuse us grandchildren with remembered adventures from his younger days. He has always been an inspiration to me.

Left: Mother and one of my aunts on a day's outing.

Above: Aunt Hilda, Father's sister. They were all very posed photographs in those days you know. Taken mostly for the family. But this one has been made into a postcard so Aunt Hilda must have used them for publicity to get engagements too.

As for me, I didn't ever really *learn* how to read music, it just had to come as I grew up. I learnt how to read music as I learnt how to read other books. I seem to have always known the notes, piano chords and so on. And of course I had to be able to read music well when Mother started me playing in orchestras when I was in my early teens.

Mother started me playing the instruments too. I can't remember it much now, it's such a long time ago, but it just seemed to happen to me naturally. She made me practise, though, but not too much. Not enough to make it a misery. Father was there to help and I suppose it was just in the family. We heard, and made, music so much that it has always been a part of my life. Not so that we would notice anything different. It was always around us.

We had musical evenings with all of us playing together and that was a lot of fun. We nearly had our own orchestra with the size of our family and often did when a few friends came to visit. Of course we did seem to have bigger families in those days. Mostly that happened when I was older but when I was a little girl I used to sit and listen while the older ones played for us. It happened on Sunday evenings usually if they hadn't gone out, and it was really very pleasant indeed.

When I was young I used to make up little songs out of advertisements by mixing them with music. Father sat and listened seriously and he thought they were great fun. I guess that was the start of it all for me. I thought that I was being clever and I sang the songs while standing at the piano. I often remember how happy we were then and how much we all shared our music. I think that it is

This photograph of Mother was taken in Wimbledon before I was born (1895). She's quite young here. She had such lovely hands. I don't know why Mother gave up playing the violin and started playing the trombone because it must have been very unusual indeed at that time. Ladies were just starting to take to the wind instruments, and the drums, and I suppose that she thought it was original and interesting. She certainly liked it.

'THE GREY LADIES' ORCHESTRA.

The Grey Ladies' Orchestra. This is a postcard and dated 30th July 1908. Aunt Julie is seated, left, with her violin and she sent the postcard to my mother. It's a very pleasant photograph I think.

terribly sad when children don't have a happy childhood. We certainly didn't have a lot of money most of the time but we did have a happy life.

Mother, who had played as a young girl, continued to play after she married Father. She didn't just stop. So if things were going all right they had two wages sometimes, and then we were doing well. But if there was a slump then nobody had work anywhere.

I remember often coming home from school to a meal of potatoes and onions made into a stew. We didn't *feel* deprived but it really couldn't have been easy for my parents sometimes. I don't think that they were paid anything special for their work, they just had to make do with what was normally paid to musicians at the time. And the worst of a musician's life is that one week you are doing jolly well and next week it's not so good. It's not at all consistent. That's why a lot of musicians don't want their children to take it up too. They worry for them. It's not easy really. But then, if you like the life you put up with that. Nearly all sorts of life has its struggles.

When I was a little girl in Luton, where Mother also played in the orchestra, there were no other children in my school whose parents were musicians or had anything to do with the theatre. They thought it was terrible really, and that we were wicked. They wouldn't have anything to do with us at first because we belonged to the 'theeeaaatre'. Nearly everybody else was involved in straw hat manufacturing. Well, all sorts of hats really but mostly made out of straw.

Many, many people were making hats at home and you could walk along the streets and see them through their basement windows. Women, and often men, were sitting at machines sewing hats. And of course you would always see them walking down the street carrying huge piles of hats – their handiwork – to the factories.

Most people in Luton earned at least some money through the hat trade so we were quite the odd ones out. It was a long time before we were invited to somebody else's house for tea which happened a lot in those days. It was a long time too, before they realised that I was quite a nice little girl after all. They were a terribly biased lot, especially there in Luton. Ardent chapel goers, you see, but still they

managed to make the theatre pay all right. It made money for quite a few years despite the way they felt about us.

When we moved back to London to live, we went to a little private school. We were older then and it just didn't seem such a problem. Of course we all lived together in London. We children, our parents who played, our grandparents who also played and when our aunts, an all-ladies group called The Biseras (see page 39), came back home from abroad, they used to stay with us too. But by then people didn't seem to take too much notice of us.

Madame Angless's Ladies' Orchestra at New Spa, Bridlington. I have no relatives in this band although I did know a cornet player, Ida Angless, who was related to the conductress.

15

In Luton the theatre closed for two months during the summer and my parents were free to take other engagements, usually by the sea, and we were always taken with them. The usual routine for musical performances was morning and afternoon sessions in the bandstand at the end of the pier. What better holiday for Mother than to relax in a deckchair with her knitting or magazine, listening to a ladies' orchestra play the strains of the latest popular airs? Often the audience was almost completely made up of ladies sewing and chatting together and it was very pleasant.

On these occasions, weather permitting, the selected few of the main orchestra would be dressed in white frocks which showed up well against the blue sky and sea. At night a full orchestral concert would be given in the pavilion. The white frocks were now shed for colourful evening dresses and the stage decorated with ferns and flowers. At the appointed hour Madame Sydney Jones would appear, baton in hand, ready to conduct the opening number: sometimes an overture from an opera or a very fine march.

A substantial library of music was required, and the musicians had to be able to read anything by sight and to play the many requests coming from the customers. The programme always included some songs, so one of the musicians had to be a trained singer, and her repertoire usually contained those favourites of the period 'Little Brown Bird Singing' and others of that ilk. There were solos from different individuals and I was often in the audience to hear my aunt play on her cornet the always in demand 'The Lost Chord' or 'I Hear You Calling Me', which were among her many. Sometimes it would be a jolly one by the trombonist which would cause much laughter.

One soloist often requested was the drummer, Dora Horsfield, known as Little Dora being rather tiny. She was a brilliant exponent of the xylophone too, and considering her diminutive stature, it was extraordinary that she had conquered these particular instruments.

At the end of these lively concerts many were the lovely bouquets or large boxes of chocolates handed up from special admirers to the different soloists, or to the whole ensemble. The applause would be doubled as Madame stepped forward to

The Grosvenor Ladies' Quintette. *None of my relatives are in this group that I know of but we must have known these musicians or we wouldn't have had the postcard. Very elegant.*

One of the larger Ladies' Orchestras. Aunt Hilda is there with her cornet but I don't know any of the other musicians. Eventually Municipal Councils became aware of the importance of these orchestras of ladies only, and were engaging them to entertain the holiday-makers and residents of large seaside resorts, and even inland, where there were fine gardens and pavilions for the public.

acknowledge and extend her thanks to the supporters. These engagements, as might be expected, were much looked forward to as summer approached.

At Ilfracombe, that lovely spot on the north Devon coast, we spent another delightful holiday. The band, composed this time of women and men, played in the pavilion on the Parade. As the number of performances were few our parents spent more time with us and many were the walks and hours on the beach. Not the golden sands of Yarmouth for building castles and making puddings in our buckets, but oh the fun of climbing the rocks and discovering the beautiful little pools left by the tides!

Dovercourt, on the East Coast, at the Alexandra Hotel, is another remembered engagement, under the direction of Miss Rose Telfer, a violinist, and member of the Scottish family of that name. She was a person of exceptionally good looks with an abundance of red hair and, because I was of the same colouring, she made a fuss of me, occasionally allowing me to sing a little ditty. My hair had to be tied with pink ribbon because it was artistic, while the blue was an abomination!

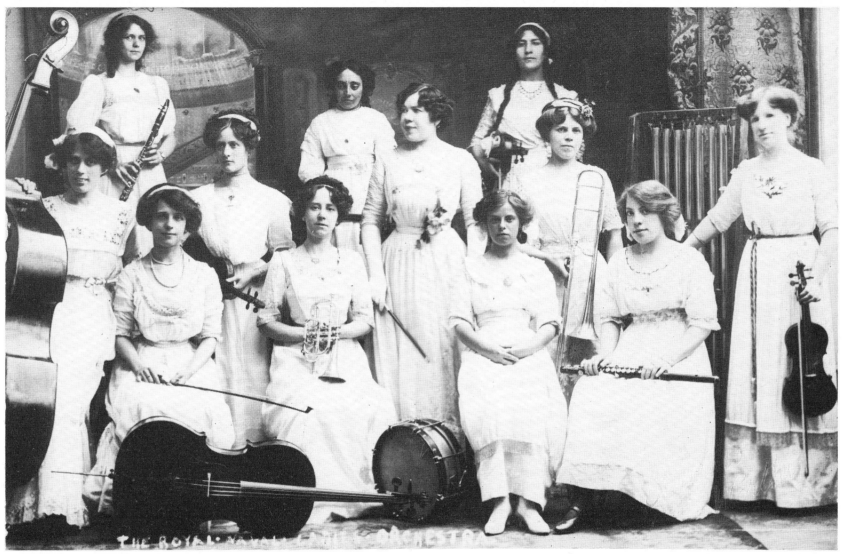

The Royal Naval Ladies' Orchestra, 26th July 1911. Conductress Madame Sydney Jones. Aunt Viola is seated second left holding the cornet and 'Little Dora' standing in the middle at the back. Madame Jones, a fine musician and excellent Chef D'Orchestra, is standing, centre, holding the baton. During the 1914 War the men from the orchestra of that fine and important Music Hall, The Coliseum, London, were called to serve and their places were responsibly filled by lady musicians, among whom were my mother on the trombone, as well as Father's sisters. It was also during this period that the Symphony Orchestras had to include many more lady players and so, again, my relatives found themselves playing under the batons of Sir Edward Elgar, who received them very kindly, and Sir Malcolm Sergeant. When the men returned from the war, however, the ladies had to give up this employment.

The Programme will consist of Selections

From the ORATORIOS of

The MESSIAH, ELIJAH, & JUDAS MACCABEUS;

And Miscellaneous Songs by Eminent Composers.

Artistes:

MDME. ALICE KENT,
MASTER BRITT,
MR. VINCENT IVES
MR. GEO. TROTMAN,
and the Central Hall Choir,

 Anglo-Saxon Orchestral Band.

Conductor - Mr. J. C. KENT.

TICKETS for TEA and CONCERT : NINEPENCE EACH.

Admission to Concert : SIXPENCE and THREEPENCE.

Tea on tables at 6 o'clock.   Doors open at 7   Commence at 7.30 p.m.

Tickets can be obtained

ow at last the ladies were making their way in the world. Trios and quartets were being engaged to play at weddings, receptions, bazaars, garden parties and even small dances. Cafe proprietors began to see their attraction and they were soon employed for tea-time dances in restaurants, then through luncheon hours and afternoons. Many hotels delighted their guests by engaging a quartet of ladies to entertain in the lounge after dinner – remember that I am speaking about a time long before television arrived, or even radio.

Later we began to see the size of the bands increasing considerably so that when the famous restauranteur, J. Lyons, opened his splended 'Maison Lyons' at Marble Arch in the West End of London in 1933, it was not surprising that the added attraction of an all-ladies' band was included. And John Barker's, the renowned large emporium in Kensington High Street, engaged a Miss Millie Bradfield to organise the music in the restaurant during luncheon and tea hours. This she did with great success for very many years.

As the ladies' orchestras were much in demand, my parents were regularly offered work in different places at the same time and they would just go and do it. It wasn't a problem really. We children might go with Mother, we wouldn't go with Father, or we would stay at home with our grandparents if they weren't away travelling themselves. It always seemed to work out somehow. If we went with Mother it was usually during a summer engagement in the school holidays, so that was never a problem.

Money could not be spared for a nurse-maid for us, so we had to take care of ourselves and I must say no harm came of it . . . but our Guardian Angel must have worked overtime! Only one unfortunate event was experienced when we were staying in a house in Caister,

This is another postcard of a woman clarinetist sent to my mother and dated 1908. I think that she was called Bee Mitton. I can't remember her although it's a wonderful photograph, don't you think? She looks utterly miserable, but is it any wonder? Fancy having to play in those clothes!

Madame Angless's Pompadour Ladies' Orchestra. They used to wear very elaborate costumes when playing for stage engagements rather than concerts and they must have been very uncomfortable sometimes.

owned by the landlady and her mother, who made us very comfortable until the supposed 'husband', a stoker aboard ship, arrived from Yarmouth Docks.

Quarrels ending in blows ensued and one night, as we were going to bed, a truly violent fight started. From our bedroom window I looked down into the kitchen to see the couple locked in combat rolling around the room. An oil lamp was burning on the table and I was frightened of it being overturned, causing a fire. With two other

Left: This is the reed section of a larger group. They had their photographs taken in separate sections like this so that people could hire them separately. I recognise the faces of some of these women as being friends of my mother and aunts but I can't remember their names. It's such a long time ago now, and I was very young then. This must have been taken about the turn of the century.

Right: The wind section. There is Mother top left, with her trombone now, and Aunt Mina next to her. Aunts Hilda and Viola are seated right in their smart white blouses and holding their cornets.

23

toddlers asleep, I sent my younger sister running up the road in her pyjamas to fetch the policeman whom we knew lived somewhere there, while I kept watch on the kitchen. By the time the officer arrived the combatants were exhausted and quiet, the worst was over, and there was nothing the policeman could do but comfort us, assuring us we were safe and that he would keep an eye on us until Mother returned.

I toured Scotland with Mother once and that's another tour that I have faint recollection of. I can remember making mud pies with the daughter of our landlady at our 'accommodation'. We went to Scotland by train, just myself and Mother, as my two sisters stayed home that time. It was quite an adventure really.

The Company used to give me small amounts of money sometimes which Mother put by and then at the end of the tour, she bought a lovely china doll. She dressed it specially with rather fine clothes, but when she handed it to me I said, 'Oh lovely', threw it up into the air, dropped it and smashed it. The very first time I had ever held it! Mother was heartbroken and cried and I was upset too.

I used to sit in the orchestra pit on a little stool at my mother's feet and listen to the music they made. At that time she was playing the trombone for the larger orchestras. They played all kinds of music depending on the type of show they had been employed for. Shows like 'Faust' and other dramas as well. Sometimes there wasn't a lot of music if they were playing for a more 'dramatic' show, just soft gentle music for pathos and harsh music for the more 'dramatic' scenes. In the interval we would all have fish and chips to eat.

Mother used to wear her own clothes and came home smelling of tobacco. It was quite a problem and it ruined your clothes. They smoked so much in the theatres. When I was older I would go down to the theatre later in the evening to see Mother and she would say, 'Oh, lovely. You've brought the fresh air with you.' You know, it was just around my clothes.

It was terribly hot and stuffy and people would come around spraying highly smelling stuff to 'purify' the air. They did that in the moving pictures too, and the sprays were really highly scented in those days. It was sickening and it's very bad for you. It was awful with the smoke but it was hard to know which was worse, the smoke or the spray. Later I always tried to travel non-smoker on the trains because I couldn't bear it.

Right. A Ladies' Orchestra at the Earls Court Exhibition, 1901. Another source of income for musicians were the grand 'Trades Exhibitions' periodically held in the largest available hall in various county or important towns. Trade exhibits were the way of advertising in those days – and very personal and lively they were too. The bands engaged for those shows kept the customers amused and interested. Mother is seated third from left, with her trombone and I have some six aunts in this thirty nine piece band. I suppose that I was only about six years old when this was taken. I only remember a small part of the day, mainly because I lost my very beautiful sunbonnet that my aunts 'The Biseras' had brought me from Paris and the rest of the day was spoiled. It blew off my head away into the lake as we children went skimming down the waterchute.

Evelyn Hardy's band at the Ideal Home Exhibition, London, 1913. Another conductress of some repute, of whom I have no photograph, was Miss Rosabelle Watson who is mentioned several times on Donald Wolfit's autobiography as having satisfactorily arranged music for his Shakespearean productions with her orchestra of ladies. And in the theatres, in those days, there were always two 'houses' a night. One Monday after the first house, at the Lewisham Hippodrome, a soubrette/comedienne, Daisy James, a popular star turn, positively refused to appear in the second house unless Ernest Beresford Kent was in the Conductor's seat. There must have been a fine row for Father was rushed by taxi from the Putney Hippodrome just in time to conduct Miss James' act.

The string section from a larger orchestra. The conductress is seated here. Again, I can only just recognise some faces.

T hen the first silent films opened, that made a tremendous difference to the musicians' work. It was splendid really. People were flocking to the cinemas to see the latest novelty and were completely enchanted. This new form of entertainment provided another source of income because the larger and grander the buildings became, so the orchestras grew in size. Sometimes there would be only women playing in the smaller cinemas but more often there would be members of both sexes.

These musicians, like my mother, who had gained so much experience in the legitimate theatre were very able to arrange suitable music for any situation required and it was a great aid to the plot. A lot of musicians got steady work like that.

I started work myself playing the piano when I was in my early teens. At first I played with Mother in the theatre orchestras for a while and then she asked if I could play the piano on my own for the first children's matinee performance of the silent films in this country. That was in a cinema in Upper Tooting in London. I must

This is me, Greta Kent, as a teenager in 1911 during my tour singing in the chorus of 'Hullo Everybody'. In my teens I also played the trombone once alongside Mother for a pageant held in the Albert Hall, London, with a Miss Watson directing. And Father must have had a goodly share of musical talent too for, at the age of only sixteen, he was invited to attend an audition given by Sir Augustus Manns, who was then selecting musicians for a large orchestra he would be conducting at the Crystal Palace. Father was engaged as one of the first violins. His professional experience was as varied as his own father's with whom he worked often. In those days musicians had to walk many miles to reach the outer suburbs to play for balls and receptions and so on, when fees would not cover the cost of a cab. So perhaps that's why we came to live in Tooting, when we returned to London in 1906 – there were all night trams for getting home late. Many musicians lived in Tooting, Balham and the surrounding areas for that very good reason.

have only been about thirteen at the time.

I used to sit and watch the picture and make up music to match the mood as it went along. It was great fun. Villain music and running music and a lot of sad moods. But it was nearly all romance – even in the children's matinees. The good man would appear and then the bad man: goodies and baddies, that sort of thing. It's fun to play music for that as there is quite a lot of variety to keep it exciting. It's a wonder I stood the noise from the children watching as the screams were fantastic. But then, I was still a child myself. I guess that if I hadn't been playing I might possibly have been watching it too.

For a small picture house a solitary pianist would be sufficient to follow the films but larger cinemas required an orchestra so, in 1908, under my mother's tuition, I went on to learn to play with the larger cinema orchestras too. This lasted a good many years, until the 'Wurlitzer' organ was installed in important Picture Palaces. Then the lone organist gave solo performances mid-programme and the great instrument was mechanically raised above the orchestra pit.

The cinema had seemed to be a God-send to musicians but, unfortunately, it ceased to be so with the introduction of the 'Talkies'. The recorded music that accompanied the soundtrack then dispensed with the need for live music altogether.

Me again, a bit more severe this time. I played for a time at the Brighton Bon Marche with a trio of other ladies. We had piano, cello and violin. And once, when I was only sixteen, I went to Rotterdam for a month to accompany a popular singer. There were just two of us ladies, myself and another, and Mother wasn't very keen about me going so far on my own. Remember, this was in 1911. It wasn't dangerous, though, and we returned safely, although the engagement itself was rather difficult. The singer we accompanied was singing in his own language and I was completely stumped. I didn't know what he was saying or where we were in the music or even what tempo I should have been playing at. Oh dear it WAS difficult but we finished the season before returning home.

My cousin Kathleen Baldwin, the flutist. Rather modern dress here so it couldn't have been taken very early.

Cousin Kathleen, again. The cellist shown here, Nell Bowden, was Godmother to all three of my girls. In the early 1920s, during my father's engagement at the Lewisham Hippodrome, the great strike of musicians occurred where he learnt a bitter and costly lesson. His idea of loyalty was to his 'Governors'. He stood by them but later, when he was forced to join the Musicians Union, his 'Governors' did not stand by him – they didn't help to pay his fines and fees. It hit him very hard, both emotionally and financially.

When I started playing it was mostly for the cinemas so I didn't go away from home very much. But I did play a bit for the live theatre and that meant travelling. I remember one time, when I was sixteen, I toured singing with the chorus of 'Hullo Everybody'. We had a Musical Director who couldn't play the piano and when he heard that I could, he asked me to play for the rehearsals. Later, in another town, the local pianist wanted some time off to get married so I played for the performances. That was great fun. But usually the performers and the musicians didn't mix much. Still, we toured and I saw a great deal of the country and had a jolly time.

I saw a lot of things that I wouldn't have seen otherwise. We travelled by train mostly and had special compartments booked just for the people touring with the show. And off we would go. I saw Stephenson's engine one night at a railway station we were passing through. We stopped and had to strike matches on the side of the carriage so that we could see it properly. It was very impressive.

Once, when we crossed to Ireland to play during the First World War, the ship zig zagged a lot during our return journey. They told us that it was because we were being chased by a submarine. I don't know if that was true but the ship certainly did zig zag more than seemed necessary at the time.

I worked for quite a few years and then married when I was twenty-three. I met my husband in the cinema where I was playing for the matinees. He worked in the cinema too and saw the prospects of cinema life, so he decided to come in right from the start working as a projectionist. He was the first to know how to run colour films in this country when they came here from America and he did quite well for himself, travelling a lot with those first colour films. He worked in the cinema all his life after that in one way or another.

I had come from a Conservative family and he was a socialist but after a few years I started to see the sense in some of the things that he was saying – I changed my attitudes about a lot of things. Once when I was talking with him, he got cross with me and said in exasperation, 'Oh, you. I liked you better when you were a Tory.' I guess that he meant when I didn't speak up for myself so much!

Right. Much later, probably about 1938-9. My sisters Winifrede on piano and Jo, accordion.

32

Other times, when he became exasperated he would say, 'Oh, you, you're just like a suffragette!' – as though that was a bad thing. I wasn't ever actually involved with what they were doing but, my goodness, I remember hearing about them. They sounded very strong.

We courted for three years and I worked during all that time but I didn't play very much after we married in 1918. He wasn't very keen about me playing and of course I soon had my own three little girls, so I stopped for quite a while. I did play a little sometimes and when I did Mother looked after my daughters for me.

I remember that once, in 1925, I took an engagement at Garon's splendid restaurant in Southend and we stayed down there for the whole season, the children and I. My husband came down for the weekends and the children had the benefit of a season living with the sea air. That was with a group of three other ladies. We wore green dresses and played at lunchtimes and that was very nice. I liked it a lot. We played light pieces. The same kind of music that we had always played: excerpts from operas, overtures, marches – the popular music of the time. We had a cello, trumpet, violin, and I played the piano.

I knew the woman who had gotten the engagement and she asked me to join them. That's one way we used to get the jobs. The conductress would contact the theatres in the area where she would like to have a season and then, after negotiations had been settled between them, she would advertise saying that she was looking for lady musicians. Of course she would also know a few that she would like to have with her so she would write to them directly and ask them first. After that there would be auditions for those who answered the advertisements and it was really quite hard if you had to do that. There were a lot of lady musicians and we all wanted work of course.

After you had played for quite a few years you got to know most of the women who worked regularly travelling around the country. So, while you didn't exactly know who was going to be in the group when you were asked or auditioned, usually when you arrived at the engagement it would be quite a reunion, meeting up with others whom you had worked with somewhere else before. It was a nice life and we had lots of laughs together. The job that I had in Southend must have paid reasonably well. Enough at least for me to be able to stay down there and pay for the accommodation for myself and my girls.

Right. This is a more recent photograph of one of the modern ladies' orchestras: The Thelma Hammond Orchestra. That's Aunt Mina on the trombone.

This was taken during a season at Scarborough. My younger sister, Jo, on the left. She worked about eight sessions there, playing the accordian and singing. A season at a place like Scarborough would last about eight weeks usually. That must be Evelyn Hardy far right, conducting.

In the meantime yet another innovation had arrived from America. The Jazz Period: a new and noisy arrangement of instruments with a great deal of syncopation in the music to which many lively dances were arranged, 'Alexander's Ragtime Band' and all that. The first 'British Syncopated Orchestra and Entertainers' appeared at Kingsway Hall, London, on Monday 1st October 1921

Another very modern group. Very jolly and happy, too.

and, according to a newspaper report, augured well for the prosperity of the latest enterprise. The writer of this report was '. . . amazed to see the inclusion of women and especially the trombonist . . .' who incidentally, happened to be my mother.

Naturally the ladies had to follow suit with this new style of music, but with a less noisy and raucous style of Jazz, for the stage and dance halls. The ancient Lyceum Theatre in London was soon converted into a vast ballroom with an all-feminine band. Among the many popular leaders of this latest craze were, I recall, Miss Thelma Hammond, Miss Hilda Ward, followed by Miss Ivy Benson with her All-Girl Dance Band. They were in great demand.

This change in entertainment did not mean that the musicians were any less accomplished than previously. For one thing much of the music had to be memorized and a new approach had to be learnt, with the syncopated rhythms, and this continued until they were gradually surplanted by the male Jazz bands.

The 'Skiffle' group, introducing rhythms on the washboard and other odd pieces of equipment, grew into what then became known as 'Pop' but all this is getting beyond my province really which ended with Miss Ivy Benson.

When I returned to playing in the mid-forties after my daughters had grown up, I didn't go back to the travelling orchestras nor did I do many seasons away from home. After the War, I took to working either at shows close to where we lived or playing for ballet and dance lessons for local school children. I enjoyed that and did it for a long time. It was exciting to see the good dancers developing and if you worked with a teacher you liked and respected it was quite rewarding. I did this for a great many years and even played in a local show up here in Suffolk where I have been living with my family since 1976.

I have been told that as I was not a well known person my memoirs would hardly be worth considering but isn't it curious that, unless one has sailed 'lone' around the Horn in a coracle, robbed a train or given birth to a test tube baby, there could not be anything worth talking or writing about?

By recording the lives of some past musicians, I hope this has been disproved. They were not classical concert artists but they were accomplished performers in the entertainment world of theatres, popular concerts, cinemas and other functions. My main theme has been the rise and fall of Ladies' Orchestras, but without mentioning the Kents and Baldwins whose names were so well known in their day, the story would not have been complete.

I have always wanted to tell what it was like to be the daughter of musicians who travelled around the country making their living and I hope that people find it interesting. For my part I think that it is important to record their lives so that we all remember what went before us.

The Biseras

This was a very popular musical act consisting of seven wind instruments and a drummer that travelled a lot around the turn of the century and a bit before. The act was lavishly dressed and produced and, being a novelty, was soon in demand especially on the Continent where they spent several years. They returned home occasionally, playing at all the best Variety Halls.

Three of my aunts – Viola, Mina and Hilda (Father's sisters) – played with The Biseras for a good many years. They toured mostly in France and Germany, appearing at large Music Halls where people would sit at tables to watch them. They wouldn't be the only act on the programme – there would be comic acts and all kinds of artists – but they were always the star performance. I don't actually remember seeing them perform but I do remember, as a small child, visiting them in the dressing rooms between shows quite a lot.

When they came back to London they would play two shows a night at different music halls and what a worry that was. There weren't any motorised vehicles then so they would have to be conveyed by horse-drawn cab from one hall to another, ready to start playing just as soon as they arrived. It must have been a strain on their nerves in case of mishap to limbs, instruments, costumes and make-up, or just arriving late for their turn, but I never heard of any accidents.

Sometimes they took part in a show, usually in the chorus, but mostly they were an act all to themselves. It was what we would call an 'intermediate' programme. Light music. They were all very good musicians as they had to play from memory. You can't walk around the stage with a music stand in front of you.

Once when they were playing at Drury Lane Theatre in London, the Musical Director Mr Jimmy Glover seemed to take a dislike to them for some unknown reason and did his best to spoil their 'turn'. He would begin by conducting their music at the correct tempo but would gradaully increase the speed until it became almost impossible for the girls to follow. One night Aunt Hilda (the leader) called them all together and told them that no matter what happened

Right: My daughters laugh when they look at these photographs now. They say, 'Just look at those costumes. 'The Biseras' were so looked after, so taken care of and protected as young ladies, and just look at them in those costumes. In some of the photographs they look more like principal boys.'

4/12/05.
Dear Em. Will send you another photograph later on, have no more left now
Love from Hilda.

A. BLANC, phot. 78, Rue de Rome-MARSEILLE

they were to follow her and ignore the conductor's beat. This they did and chaos ensued. Needless to say such a thing never occurred again and The Biseras continued in peace and popularity.

The group was managed by Mr and Madame Biseras who went everywhere with them and looked after them very well, treating them as their own daughters. I remember that Madame Biseras always used to carry a little dog under her arm, which was all the vogue in those days. She didn't play an instrument herself. The costumes for The Biseras were mostly chosen by Mr and Madame Biseras and what an imagination they must have had.

In one theatre in Germany, it was discovered that, through some error in the contract, the troupe was expected to 'entertain' gentlemen after the last performance. The suggestion was absurd and angry scenes followed. Management made the excuse that the girls were not qualified musicians and legal action was taken. Back to London came the eight Biseras to attend the hearing, with Aunt Hilda sitting all day with her cornet 'at the ready' in the event of having to show her skill. This did not become necessary as the case was settled out of court finally.

Mr and Madame Biseras were a kindly couple and the group was very happy. But then they tried to change the act and my aunts wouldn't do what was being asked of them. I think they wanted the musicians to climb up a pole playing the trombone or some such silly idea and so my aunts left and the group finally split up.

They played abroad on their own for a short time but then returned to London and went on to play with other orchestras around the country. They still played together often. Mina and Hilda didn't marry. Viola did but was widowed quite early so she just kept playing. Her husband was a regular soldier and he occasionally played the viola as well. When he came out of the army he played more regularly. Mina and Hilda supported themselves with the money they earned from playing.

Greta Kent
July 1983

Left. I can remember looking forward to my aunts returning home after they had been touring abroad . . . they always had such exciting tales to tell us and little presents to give us. Nougat and suchlike and fine sunbonnets from Paris, which we thought were very smart as they were the latest fashion. They talked about the theatres they played at, how the audiences clapped and how they always had a lot of fun and laughed a lot. It was exciting having aunts who travelled so much abroad – they were very popular.

Biseras. Mol. Crignal

A. BLANC, phot. 78, Rue de Rome-MARSEILLE

One unusual number introduced by this company of musicians was the eight of them playing the 'natural trumpets' (bugles) which I can only describe as resembling the trumpets used by heralds. I hope I am correct in this for, anyway, it was an item which 'brought the house down', that theatrical term for success, as was Aunt Hilda's rendering of The Posthorn Gallop on that particular instrument.

In Paris at the Folies Bergeres, being young English girls in France for the first time, they were unmercifully teased by the French show girls who were used to walking around nude, making such remarks to them as "Oh la la, Engleeeesh – shocking", which must have caused much embarrassment to the modesty of these inexperienced girls.

The Eight Risera's Original

A.BLANC, phot. 78, Rue de Rome-MARSEILLE

At last, after several years of successful engagements both at home here in England and on the Continent, 'The Biseras' were disbanded – to make way for new ideas – so they were not too regretful.

Coda

Following my first book of memories, 'Luton from the Wings' (printed and published by the Borough of Luton), a record of my childhood days in Luton and the Grand Theatre, I have considered the possibility of the spirit of Grandfather J.C. Kent encouraging me throughout. Spiritualism was in vogue in the 1880s and his diaries show that he played often at these meetings. They were great musical events, starting with selections from popular classical music followed by sacred songs and recitations. The evening always closed with a hymn, and a dated edition of 'The Medium' says, 'There were no such grand musical efforts being made by spiritualists in any other part of the country.'

Grandfather's daughter, who used to hold seances, claimed that 'Father always comes in a jovial mood', so perhaps he has been enjoying this written account of his family's exploits.

Also, I must mention a comment that I read once from that renowned diarist, Samuel Pepys, himself a passionate lover of music. He wrote, 'I went down to Greenwich to eat and drink and heard music at the 'Globe', and saw the simple notion that is there, of a woman with a rod in her hand, keeping time with the music while it played, which is simple methinks.'

What would he make of the achievement of the 'women with a rod in their hands' three hundred odd years later?!

🐈 Sheba Feminist Publishers

Sheba is an independent feminist publishing co-operative which produces books by and about women. Our list includes titles under the following headings: fiction and poetry, sex and sexuality, books for younger readers, and on women in other countries, feminist theory and visual books. All our titles are available from bookshops, or direct from *Sheba Feminist Publishers*, 488, Kingsland Road, London E8. Please add 45p per volume for p&p. Send SAE to our address for our complete catalogue of books, postcards and posters.

Sheba backlist of visual books

Our Own Freedom, *Maggie Murray, Buchi Emecheta*

Women in Africa today – 90 photographs by Maggie Murray with an introduction by Buchi Emecheta, the well-known Nigerian novelist.

'This is a powerful and convincing record, the combination of photographs and text unfolding the realities of women's experience more immediately and effectively than a purely "academic" analysis could do.' *Campaigns Bulletin, Third World First*
February 1982 £3.75 USA$8.95 112 pp 219×200mm ISBN 0 907179 09 06

Heavy Periods, *Fanny Tribble*

Originally self-published in 1979, these hilarious strip cartoons were immediately snapped up, and sold out very quickly. Now in reprint from *Sheba, Heavy Periods* unearths our inner doubts and conflicts and makes us laugh at them. Look inside and you will be hooked.

'. . . the funny side of feminism . . .' *The Artful Reporter*
'Fanny Tribble's strips show up and send up the contradictions of getting through life as a feminist.' *Guardian*
'Illustrates the endless contradictions of a raised consciousness . . . painfully funny especially on sexuality.' *Spare Rib*
May 1983 £1.50 $3.95 32pp 175×245mm ISBN 0 907179 18 5

Funny Trouble, *Fanny Tribble*

The follow-up to Fanny Tribble's *Heavy Periods* shows Fanny five years on – the hot water bottles are men and babies now, but the bewildered Fanny is still trying to make sense out of . . . sex and celibacy, allotments and relationships.

'A kind of 80's Candide – revealing both herself and us . . . in the sumptious complexity of our . . . confusions.' *City Limits*
November 1982 £1.50 $3.95 48pp 174×246mm ISBN 0 907179 15 0

Sourcream, *Jo Nesbitt, Liz Mackie, Lesley Ruda, Christine Roche*

This country's highly successful first feminist cartoon book, now in third reprint.
April 1980 £1.75 USA$4.95 96pp 150×229mm ISBN 0 907179 00 2

Sourcream 2, *Cathy Porter, Carry Ackroyd, Pink Jane, Janis Goodman, Susannah Smith, Ann-Marie Blatchford, Viv Quillan, Fanny Tribble, Fiona Scott, Janet Stein, Laura Coutts, Catriona Sinclair, Rosalind Scott*

'*Sourcream 2*, is a rich dollop of feminist humour and a follow-up to last year's *Sourcream*, that excellent collection of women's cartoons.' *Observer*
December 1981 £1.75 USA$4.95 96pp 229×150mm ISBN 0 907179 10 X